GREAT JOBS

Great Jobs in Engineering

Peggy J. Parks

ReferencePoint Press®

San Diego, CA

About the Author

Peggy J. Parks loves being an author and has written dozens of educational books on a wide variety of topics for teens and young adults. She holds a bachelor's degree from Aquinas College in Grand Rapids, Michigan, where she graduated magna cum laude. Parks lives in Muskegon, Michigan, a town she says inspires her writing because of its location on the shores of beautiful Lake Michigan.

Printed in the United States

For more information, contact:
ReferencePoint Press, Inc.
PO Box 27779
San Diego, CA 92198
www.ReferencePointPress.com

Picture Credits:

Cover: nd3000/Shutterstock.com
6: Maury Aaseng
13: goodluz/Shutterstock.com
37: Kaspars Grinvalds/Shutterstock.com
44: seyomedo/Shutterstock.com
62: GaudiLab/Shutterstock.com

LIBRARY OF CONGRESS CATALOGING-IN-PUBLICATION DATA

Name: Parks, Peggy J., 1951–author.
Title: Great Jobs in Engineering/by Peggy J. Parks.
Description: San Diego, CA: ReferencePoint Press, Inc., 2019. | Series: Great Jobs | Audience: Grade 9 to 12. | Includes bibliographical references and index.
Identifiers: LCCN 2018040174 (print) | LCCN 2018044591 (ebook) | ISBN 9781682825228 (eBook) | ISBN 9781682825211 | ISBN 9781682825211 (hardback)
Subjects: LCSH: Engineers—Vocational guidance—Juvenile literature.
Classification: LCC TA157 (ebook) | LCC TA157 .P29 2019 (print) | DDC 620.0023—dc23
LC record available at https://lccn.loc.gov/2018040174

Contents

Introduction

The Problem Solvers

Engineers are people who solve problems for a living. These problems can be incredibly diverse, ranging from the need for medical devices that save human lives to buildings that can withstand earthquakes to methods of reducing pollution so people have clean drinking water. It is up to engineers to analyze such problems and figure out the best way to solve them. "You take a problem and you look at it from every direction," design engineer Kevin King says in an article on the Rice University website. "Then you come up with various solutions, and right away you start crossing them off the list. That's what engineers do."

The Engineering Mindset

Because problem solving is such a fundamental part of being an engineer, people who choose to pursue a career in engineering are typically those who enjoy solving problems. Most engineers say that even as children they were intrigued by how things worked. To satisfy their curiosity, they took apart toys, electronic gadgets, and even small household appliances to examine their working mechanisms.

Clara Wright, who is an engineer with the National Aeronautics and Space Administration's (NASA) Kennedy Space Center, has always loved problem solving. From a very young age she enjoyed jigsaw puzzles, even those that were difficult. "I used to really like making jigsaw puzzles—1,000-piece to 2,000-piece puzzles—and I liked to see how things fit together and came apart," Wright says in an article on the NASA website. By the time Wright was in high school, her interest in problem solving had turned into a passion. That, along with excelling in science and math, led to her enrollment in her school's math, science, and engineering program. Ultimately, she decided that a career in engineering was the perfect fit for her.

A Vast Array of Choices

Wright is a materials engineer, which is one of many engineering specialties. Materials engineers develop and test materials that are used to make all kinds of products, from computer chips and aircraft wings to smartphones and heavy machinery. Aerospace engineers design aircraft, spacecraft, satellites, and missile systems. Civil engineers, who account for the most jobs of all engineering specialties, play an essential role in the development and maintenance of infrastructure projects. Infrastructure is the vast underlying structure that is essential for a country to function. Roads, bridges, dams, railways, subways, and airports are all part of the infrastructure, as are the power supply and systems that provide water and sewage treatment. "Most people don't realize that civil engineers build the infrastructure that touches everyone's lives in one way or another," says civil engineer Jennifer Chehab. Her comments appear in a brochure for the engineering firm Fleis & VandenBrink.

Engineers may specialize in a number of other areas as well. Mechanical engineers, for instance, design, build, and test tools, engines, and machines of a wide variety, from electricity generators and steam turbines to air-conditioning systems and elevators. Structural engineers design and build bridges and other load-bearing structures. Industrial engineers specialize in eliminating waste by improving production processes. Electrical engineers design, develop, test, and supervise the manufacture of electric motors, radar and navigation systems, communication systems, and equipment that generates power. Health and safety engineers design systems and procedures that protect public health. Also focused on health are biomedical engineers, who address medical needs by designing equipment, devices, and computer systems that are specifically used by health care professionals.

These engineering types represent only a fraction of the numerous engineering specialties and subspecialties. In fact, the field of

Great Jobs in Engineering

Occupation	Minimum Educational Requirement	2017 Median Pay
Aerospace engineer	Bachelor's degree	$113,030
Chemical engineer	Bachelor's degree	$102,160
Drafter	Associate's degree	$54,170
Environmental engineering technician	Associate's degree	$50,230
Environmental engineer	Bachelor's degree	$86,800
Health and safety engineer	Bachelor's degree	$88,510
Industrial engineering technician	Associate's degree	$54,280
Landscape architect	Bachelor's degree	$65,760
Marine engineer and naval architect	Bachelor's degree	$90,970
Materials engineer	Bachelor's degree	$94,610
Petroleum engineer	Bachelor's degree	$132,280
Surveying and mapping technician	High school diploma or equivalent	$43,340
Surveyor	Bachelor's degree	$61,140

Source: Bureau of Labor Statistics, *Occupational Outlook Handbook*, 2018. www.bls.gov.

engineering is so diverse that it offers more career choices than most any other professional field. Equally diverse are the places where engineers work. Depending on their specialty, they might be employed by manufacturing operations, government agencies (federal, state, or local), major utility or energy companies, aircraft corporations, universities, hospitals, research facilities, and specialty engineering firms, as well as countless others. "Engineers work everywhere—in big cities, small cities, rural communities, even remote wilderness areas," chemical engineer Kristen Svec writes in the Burns & McDonnell career blog. "Some of us work in an office setting, some in refineries, power plants, factories, research labs and even Disney World. Some work outdoors and some in outer space!" This variety, says Svec, is one of the best parts of being an engineer. "The opportunities and possibilities are endless—and it's one of the things I love most about my career."

A Bright Future

Opportunities are many for those who choose an engineering career. According to the Bureau of Labor Statistics (BLS), engineers will be in high demand over the coming years. Their professional expertise and skills will be needed in all types of areas, including robotics, renewable energy, oil and gas extraction, and the rebuilding of America's aging infrastructure. The field of engineering as a whole is expected to grow by 7 percent through the year 2026, which the BLS says is about average for all occupations.

Growth projections vary a great deal based on specialty, however. The BLS projects double-digit growth for some specialties, such as cartography, which is expected to grow 19 percent by 2026. Sometimes known as cartographic engineers, cartographers conceive, design, and produce maps. Other engineering specialties with higher-than-average growth potential are petroleum engineers, with 15 percent expected growth by 2026; civil engineers, at 11 percent; and industrial engineers, at 10 percent.

Career experts, education counselors, and people already working in the engineering fields strongly urge young people to consider one of the many engineering careers. Aside from diverse specialties from which to choose, generous salaries, and a positive future outlook, engineering offers a chance to do work that benefits society. "We get to work on projects that change the world," says Svec, "and there's no better feeling than knowing you're making a difference."

Civil Engineer

What Does a Civil Engineer Do?

Day after day civil engineers are faced with tough, challenging problems, and they must figure out how to solve those problems. They envision, design, build, supervise, and maintain the infrastructure on which the public depends. "They literally shape the world people live in," civil engineer Mark Swink says in a Whole Building Design Guide article.

Civil engineers work on a staggering array of projects. When a new apartment building is planned, they are involved from the very beginning. When a city outgrows its airport and needs a larger one, civil engineers get the process rolling. When an aging water-treatment system no longer meets the needs of a community's residents, civil engineers design and build a better system. When studies show that a new road or highway is needed, civil engineers participate in all phases, from initial designs and construction up to the day the road finally opens. As civil engineer Emily Munday writes in the Society of Women Engineers blog, "The absolute best part of my job is being able to drive over a road that I designed!"

At a Glance

Civil Engineer

Minimum Educational Requirements
Bachelor's degree

Personal Qualities
Leadership and decision-making skills; strong math, writing, and problem-solving skills; organization skills; speaking skills

Certification and Licensing
Not required for entry-level positions

Working Conditions
A variety of indoor and outdoor locations

Salary Range
About $54,150 to more than $138,000

Number of Jobs
About 303,500 in 2016

Future Job Outlook
Growth of 11 percent through 2026

Civil engineers often specialize. Construction engineers, for example, are in charge of projects within the construction industry, such as designing buildings, bridges, or airports. Transportation engineers plan and design roads, railways, and mass-transit systems like subways and elevated trains. Geotechnical engineers are concerned with what lies beneath the earth's surface. Before anything is constructed, whether it is an airport runway, skyscraper, cell phone tower, or city street, geotechnical engineers conduct testing to determine the composition of materials beneath the construction site. Once this testing is complete, contractors use the results to best prepare the site for building.

Structural engineering is another civil engineering specialty. Structural engineers are responsible for stabilizing the framework of structures so they remain upright rather than collapsing in a heap of rubble. In a paper available through its website, the National Council of Structural Engineers Associations says that structural engineers "design the structure to resist forces from gravity, earthquakes, high winds, water, soil, collisions and blast explosions."

Whatever their specialty, civil engineers have innumerable responsibilities. During a project's early planning phases, civil engineers analyze survey reports, maps, and other types of relevant data. These analyses give them a good understanding of the project and what it will entail. They review government regulations, as well as any potential environmental issues that could cause problems during construction and after. They prepare cost estimates, as well as work with many kinds of software. They oversee construction of projects, monitor progress, and address any problems that crop up along the way. When a project has been completed, civil engineers are involved with ongoing maintenance and repair.

Civil engineers are also called on when natural disasters strike. When, for example, a hurricane damages or destroys roads, public utility systems, railways, bridges, or buildings, civil engineers help with rebuilding. And in the aftermath of a natural disaster, civil engineers conduct studies of damage, which can help a community be better prepared for future weather disasters. This was the case in 2017 after Hurricane Harvey slammed into the Texas coast. The massive hurricane caused catastrophic wind damage and flooding to coastal areas as well as to the city of Houston. Afterward, a team of civil engineers traveled to southeastern Texas to assess erosion impact on the coastline. The engineers spent four days investigating fourteen sites where structures had failed. Based on their findings, they made recommendations for improved hurricane preparedness.

How Do You Become a Civil Engineer?

Education

A career in civil engineering requires a bachelor's degree from a college or university whose engineering program is accredited by the Accreditation Board for Engineering Technology (ABET). Aspiring civil engineers will take a variety of classroom courses with heavy emphasis on math and science. A typical curriculum will include subjects such as calculus, physics, chemistry, civil engineering design, structural design, and soil mechanics, along with other required courses and electives.

According to the Bureau of Labor Statistics (BLS), about one out of five civil engineers go on to earn a master's degree. Advanced education is not a requirement, but career counselors say that it definitely has advantages. Master's-level civil engineers are often given more responsibility and are more likely to be chosen for leadership positions than those with a bachelor's degree.

Certification

Although licensure is not required for entry-level positions, employers typically expect civil engineers to earn their Professional Engineering (PE) license. (For those who work on public projects, the PE license is required.) Once they have earned a bachelor's degree from an ABET-accredited engineering program, civil engineers must do the following to be licensed and certified as a PE: earn a passing score on the Fundamentals of Engineering exam, work for four years under a licensed engineer, and pass the PE exam.

Each state has its own licensing board that issues PE licenses to engineers who have met all the qualifications. In many cases employers offer assistance with preparing and filing application forms, paying any required fees, and sponsoring review courses.

Volunteer Work and Internships

Aspiring civil engineers can participate in events that are designed to give young people a firsthand glimpse at what these professionals do. One example is the Student Days Conference, which is held annually in San Diego, California. Sponsored by the American Society of Civil Engineers (ASCE), the conference enables young people to get to know other engineering students, participate in challenging team events, and network with professional engineers who could potentially be future employers.

Internships are common for young people who plan to become civil engineers. These are typically paid and take place during summers while engineering students are on break from college. Internships can be invaluable for young people, providing them with opportunities to gain hands-on experience in their chosen career.

Skills and Personality

Civil engineers need a wide variety of skills, with problem-solving expertise among the most important. They must be analytical and detail oriented, because engineering projects involve countless details. They must be skilled in math and science and able to think logically. Being tech savvy is essential because civil engineers use a variety of computer programs to do their jobs. And decision-making skills are an absolute must.

Being curious and imaginative are very important personal qualities for civil engineers, since they need to think up solutions to so many types of problems. Because they work with all kinds of people, from fellow engineers to clients and construction workers, civil engineers must have good interpersonal skills and get along well with others. Good communication skills are essential, including the ability to listen effectively and speak well. Being a team player is important, as is the ability to work independently.

On the Job

Employers

According to the BLS, civil engineers held 303,500 jobs during 2016. Nearly half were employed by private engineering firms, ranging from small firms with only a few employees to mega companies with thousands of engineers on their payrolls. In a career brochure published online, the ASCE states, "At smaller firms, civil engineers have the opportunity to work on numerous varied projects, design challenges, and management-related activities. At larger firms, they have the opportunity to focus on specific projects, design expertise, and business management, depending on the core competence of the firm."

Most civil engineers who are not employed by private companies are in the public sector, working for local, state, or federal government agencies. Another 6 percent work for construction companies.

Working Conditions

Most civil engineers work full time, with about one-third working more than forty hours per week. They work hard, and if a project is running behind schedule, this will likely require even longer work hours. According to the BLS, civil engineers who direct projects may need to spend extra time working to monitor their progress, make sure specifications and design requirements are met, and guarantee that the projects are complete by the deadline.

Civil engineers may work inside or outside, depending on what needs to be done. During the early phases of a project, when civil engineers are reviewing and finalizing plans, creating designs, and preparing cost estimates, they typically work in an office. When construction starts, such as building a new electrical power plant, sports arena, parking lot, or wind farm, they often spend considerable time outside at the project site. As one civil engineer told the *Princeton Review*, "Sometimes you live out there for two or three days at a time." By being on-site, civil engineers can coordinate construction, monitor the progress of a project, and resolve problems on the spot.

Civil engineers look over plans at a job site. These professionals are involved in many aspects of construction, including new building design and development and the rebuilding of structures damaged by weather disasters.

Earnings

Civil engineering is known as a career that pays exceptionally well. The BLS states that the median wage for civil engineers in May 2017 was $84,770 per year. This represents an average between the lowest-paid 10 percent, who earned under $54,150 annually, and the highest-paid 10 percent, who earned more than $138,110. Civil engineers who work for the federal government earned an average of $93,820, followed by local governments at $90,280. Private engineering firms paid an annual average salary of $83,970, while state government agencies paid $82,050. Among civil engineers who work for construction firms, the average yearly wage was $78,130. According to the *U.S. News & World Report* 2017 Best Engineering Jobs ranking, the best-paying states for civil engineers are Alaska, California, Texas, and New Jersey, as well as the District of Columbia.

Opportunities for Advancement

Once civil engineers have worked in a job for four or five years and earned their PE license, they are well on their way to a solid engineering career. They may be promoted to more senior positions, such as project managers or other jobs with increased responsibility. Many return to school to earn a master's degree or PhD, which often results in better promotion opportunities and higher salary. Holding an advanced degree also allows civil engineers to teach at the college level, if that is a direction they want to pursue.

What Is the Future Outlook for Civil Engineers?

Engineering is considered a hot career field, and skilled civil engineers are in demand all over the world. The BLS predicts that employment of civil engineers will grow by 11 percent through 2026, which is faster than the average for all occupations. This amounts to more than thirty-two thousand new jobs for civil engineers in the not-so-distant future.

Much of this future growth, according to the BLS, is attributed to aging (and some say crumbling) infrastructure in the United States. Civil engineers will be needed to manage projects to rebuild, repair, and upgrade bridges, roads, highways, dams, airports, levees, water and sewage treatment systems, and buildings of most every shape and size. Civil engineer K.P. Reddy discusses this in an article titled "Civil Engineers Rule the Future!," which appears on the website of his company, the Combine. Reddy writes, "Our current infrastructure is very, very old. . . . Whose job is it to design, create, and build new, better infrastructure? Civil engineers."

Find Out More

American Society of Civil Engineers (ASCE)
1801 Alexander Bell Dr.
Reston, VA 20191
website: www.asce.org

Founded in 1852, the ASCE is the United States' oldest engineering society. The website offers education and career information, access to trade publications such as *Civil Engineering* magazine, and the most critical issues facing civil engineers today and in the future.

Earthquake Engineering Research Institute (EERI)
499 Fourteenth St., Suite 220
Oakland, CA 94612
website: www.eeri.org

The EERI is a technical society of civil engineers, scientists, and other professionals devoted to reducing the risks associated with earthquakes. The website offers information about student activities, public policy, current projects, news articles, and a link to the *Pulse* e-newsletter.

EngineerGirl
National Academy of Engineering
500 Fifth St. NW, Room 1047
Washington, DC 20001
website: www.engineergirl.org

The EngineerGirl website is designed to bring public attention to the many opportunities that engineering represents for girls and women, since women remain underrepresented in the engineering field. The website is a valuable resource for all kinds of information about engineering careers, including civil engineering.

Ultimate Civil Engineering Directory
website: www.tenlinks.com/engineering/civil

This online directory is packed with information about civil engineering and related topics. It offers information about bridges, building codes, dams and reservoirs, tall buildings and structures, and many other resources.

Petroleum Engineer

What Does a Petroleum Engineer Do?

Petroleum engineering involves the exploration, extraction, and production of petroleum. Petroleum exists in liquid form as crude oil and in vapor form as natural gas. It is found deep in the ground within pockets of porous rock known as reservoirs. It is up to petroleum engineers to design and develop ways to extract petroleum from the ground—an extraordinary challenge, since the reservoirs are buried anywhere from 3,000 feet to 20,000 feet (914.4 m to 6,096 m) beneath the surface of the earth.

Petroleum engineers receive scientific data from geologists, who identify areas that are likely to have buried reservoirs. A thorough understanding of this geological data is essential, since the success or failure of a drilling operation depends on it. "You can't put a human being two miles into the earth," says petroleum engineer Russell Parker in a 2017 *U.S. News & World Report* article. "You have to do all of your work with the data that you take . . . there are so many unknowns that you have to deal with." Based on careful analyses of data, petroleum engineers determine the best drilling methods

At a Glance

Petroleum Engineer

Minimum Educational Requirements
Bachelor's degree

Personal Qualities
Analytical skills, creativity, math and problem-solving skills, interpersonal skills

Certification and Licensing
Not required for entry-level positions

Working Conditions
Indoors or at drilling and well sites

Salary Range
About $74,400 to more than $208,000

Number of Jobs
About 33,700 in 2016

Future Job Outlook
Growth of 15 percent through 2026

to use and then design and build the needed equipment. Because of the unknowns, including whether the reservoir contains enough petroleum to make it worth drilling, a series of test wells are drilled. If the tests indicate a productive well, the drilling operation will begin—and can last for several months to as long as several years.

Along with designing and developing equipment to drill new wells, petroleum engineers are responsible for ongoing maintenance on existing wells. They troubleshoot problems, figure out what has gone wrong, and redesign and build new equipment if needed. Petroleum engineer Brandon Pronk, who works for a large North American oil company, says fixing broken wells is what he enjoys most about his job. On the knowledge-sharing platform Quora, he writes about his favorite task: "I love troubleshooting wells that aren't pumping, making an educated guess on what went wrong, then sending a rig to pull the equipment and see if I'm right." Pronk is a production engineer, which is one specialty of petroleum engineering. Production engineers specialize in a number of tasks, such as monitoring well production and fixing problems that occur. Also, production engineers figure out ways to make wells more productive by coaxing more oil or gas from them. A closely related specialty is the reservoir engineer, whose job is to estimate how much oil or gas can be recovered by closely studying the reservoirs' characteristics. Reservoir engineers determine which methods would work best for extraction and estimate how much it will cost. Drilling engineers figure out the best way to drill wells while keeping in mind factors such as cost and efficiency, safety, and drilling processes that cause minimal disturbance to the environment.

Another petroleum engineering specialty is the job of completions engineer. This engineer focuses on the best way to finish building wells so that oil and gas deposits flow upward from the deep underground reservoirs. Completions engineers could recommend several different techniques, one of which is hydraulic fracturing, more commonly known as fracking. Completions engineers supervise the entire procedure, which begins after the well has been drilled. Fluids—mostly water with sand, chemicals, and abrasives added—are pumped into the ground at extremely high pressure. This is powerful enough to fracture the surrounding rock, creating cracks through which oil and gas can flow to the surface.

How Do You Become a Petroleum Engineer?

Education

Becoming a petroleum engineer starts with earning a bachelor's degree, preferably from a college or university whose engineering program has been accredited by the Accreditation Board for Engineering Technology (ABET). Students will typically major in petroleum engineering, although some choose another type of engineering or one of the earth sciences (such as geophysics). Course work will be challenging, with classes in geology, geophysics, chemistry, thermodynamics, fluid dynamics, and physics, among others. Along with classroom courses, students will take part in laboratory work and field studies.

Petroleum engineers often go on to earn advanced degrees. This can be a job-seeking advantage, since many companies that employ petroleum engineers choose those with the highest level of education. In a 2017 survey by the Society of Petroleum Engineers (SPE), nearly 45 percent of respondents said they had education beyond a bachelor's degree.

Certification

Licensure is not required for entry-level petroleum engineer positions, but becoming a Professional Engineer (PE) is highly recommended. Once aspiring petroleum engineers earn a bachelor's degree from an ABET-accredited engineering program, there are three steps they must follow to be licensed and certified as a PE: take the Fundamentals of Engineering exam and earn a passing score, work for four years under a PE licensed engineer, and pass the PE exam.

An additional certification is available from the SPE. To earn this credential, petroleum engineers must be members of the society, have a minimum of four years' experience in engineering, and pass a certification exam that covers a number of specialized topics. Once they are certified, the SPE requires petroleum engineers to participate in sixteen hours of continued professional development activities each year.

Volunteer Work and Internships

There are many opportunities for aspiring petroleum engineers to participate in volunteer work. By joining the SPE, students can learn about that organization's volunteer opportunities. Colleges often have their own SPE student chapters. Through this involvement, students may participate in many different activities, such as mentoring programs, webinars, site visits, and technical conferences.

Internships have been hailed as an invaluable step toward a petroleum engineering career. They are usually paid and can provide aspiring petroleum engineers with valuable hands-on experience in their chosen field. There are other benefits too, such as the possibility of transitioning into a job at the company for which they intern. In fact, internships are one of the leading ways companies find and hire new petroleum engineering staff. In an article that appears on its website, Gate Energy writes, "Think of it as a really long interview, after which you've proved that you are a capable and hardworking employee. Just as you're giving the industry and the company a trial run, they're doing the same for you."

Skills and Personality

Problem-solving skills are among the most crucial skills for petroleum engineers. As one veteran petroleum engineer told the *Princeton Review*, "You've got to be able to see problems before they happen, otherwise you're right in the middle of them." Analytical skill is also essential, as is critical thinking and the ability to accept failure—because there are no guarantees when drilling for oil and gas, and occasional failure is part of the job.

Petroleum engineers work with all kinds of people, from other engineers and scientists to oil and gas field workers. So strong interpersonal skills and the ability to get along with others are necessary. For the same reason, petroleum engineers must be team players, since oil and gas production takes an entire team of people. Because they must often communicate their concepts and solutions to problems in writing, they need strong writing skills, as well as good verbal communication skills.

On the Job

Employers

Most petroleum engineers are employed by energy companies. During the 2017 SPE survey, more than 56 percent of respondents said they work for some type of oil and gas company. The remainder work either for service or manufacturing companies or for energy consulting firms. Because many of these companies have global operations, it is not uncommon for petroleum engineers to work in countries outside the United States.

Working Conditions

Depending on their specific job, the work life of a petroleum engineer can be exhilarating as well as challenging. More than 90 percent work full time, with about one out of three working more than forty hours per week. They spend some of their time in an office doing paperwork, working with computers on design concepts, and participating in meetings. Those who are employed by large oil and gas companies must also work at drilling sites, often for extended periods of time. Most of these sites are onshore, where wells are dug on land.

Drilling operations can also be located offshore, where wells are drilled into the ocean floor. Petroleum engineers assigned to these offshore operations do their work from an oil rig floating several hundred miles from shore and tethered to the seabed. The Gulf of Mexico is home to the second-largest number of offshore rigs in the world. One of them is Shell's massive Olympus rig and drilling operation, which is 130 miles (209.2 km) from the coast of New Orleans, Louisiana. The rig is forty stories tall and weighs more than 120,000 tons (108,862 metric tons).

Workers, including petroleum engineers, usually spend two weeks straight on the rig. Then a helicopter flies them back to shore, and they are off for two weeks. A petroleum engineer who posted on the discussion website Reddit described life on an oil rig, which he emphasizes is far more risky than working at onshore drilling operations. "The stakes are just so much higher," he says. One grave risk is to the environment, such as the *Deepwater Horizon* accident in April 2010. Along with causing catastrophic environmental damage in the Gulf of Mexico, it killed eleven workers. "If there is a blowout, there is nowhere to run," the engineer writes. Yet despite the risks and challenges, most petroleum engineers surveyed say that they enjoy their jobs very much. "I really love what I do," says the engineer in the Reddit posting.

Earnings

Petroleum engineers are well compensated for the work they do. In fact, the Bureau of Labor Statistics (BLS) reports that they are the highest paid of all engineering disciplines. As of May 2017 the median annual wage for petroleum engineers was $132,280, with the highest-paid 10 percent earning more than $200,000 per year. The 2017 SPE survey found higher earnings, with the average annual salary for petroleum engineers nearly $195,000.

Opportunities for Advancement

Petroleum engineers must work in a job for four or five years, gain knowledge about the petroleum industry, and obtain hands-on experience, and work hard to prove themselves. After five years or so, depending on how well they have performed, they may be assigned more responsibility. They could rise to the level of supervisor, in charge of teams of engineers and technicians. Some become engineering managers or move into other types of managerial positions. As they move up the career ladder, petroleum engineers will see their salary increase. According to the 2017 SPE survey, top management in petroleum engineering earned more than $388,000 per year.

What Is the Future Outlook for Petroleum Engineers?

The future looks promising for aspiring petroleum engineers. Because of the growing emphasis on renewable energy, it is a common belief that the need for these professionals will decline in the coming years—but that is not necessarily the case. Experts predict that the demand for petroleum engineers will grow. According to the BLS, employment of petroleum engineers is projected to increase 15 percent by 2026, which is much faster than the average for all jobs. This translates to more than five thousand new jobs for aspiring petroleum engineers.

Find Out More

American Institute of Mining, Metallurgical, and Petroleum Engineers (AIME)
12999 E. Adam Aircraft Cir.
Englewood, CO 80112
website: www.aimehq.org

The AIME, which has more than 145,000 members, is a professional association for mining and metallurgy. The website links to industry publications, as well as other sites that provide additional information about petroleum engineering and related topics.

National Ocean Industries Association (NOIA)
1120 G St. NW, Suite 900
Washington, DC 20005
website: www.noia.org

With nearly three hundred member companies, the NOIA represents America's offshore energy industry. Its website offers much information about issues relevant to aspiring petroleum engineers, including booklets about energy production, a section on environmental issues related to drilling, research, and news articles.

Oil & Gas Engineering

website: www.oilandgaseng.com

Oil & Gas Engineering is a media group that serves engineers and other professionals by providing information on new technologies, products, and processes that support oil and gas production. Many articles of interest to petroleum engineers are available on its website.

Society of Petroleum Engineers (SPE)

222 Palisades Creek Dr.
Richardson, TX 75080
website: www.spe.org

The SPE is a professional association whose members are involved in energy resource development and production. Its website offers industry publications such as *Oil and Gas Facilities* and the *Journal of Petroleum Technology*, as well as news articles, technical papers, and a section especially for students.

US Energy Information Administration (EIA)

1000 Independence Ave. SW
Washington, DC 20585
website: www.eia.gov

An agency of the US Department of Energy, the EIA seeks to promote sound policy making and public understanding regarding energy and its interaction with the economy and environment. A wealth of information about petroleum products and petroleum engineering can be found on its website.

Industrial Engineer

What Does an Industrial Engineer Do?

At the heart of an industrial engineer's job is figuring out better ways to get things done. There is always room for improvement even in the most successful, profitable organizations, and that is where industrial engineers come in. They work for all kinds of industries, including manufacturing; service industries such as hospitality, travel, and entertainment; health care; and finance, among a host of others. These sorts of industries depend on industrial engineers to come up with ways to help them save money and make their operations run more efficiently.

> **At a Glance**
>
> **Industrial Engineer**
>
> **Minimum Educational Requirements**
> Bachelor's degree
>
> **Personal Qualities**
> Creativity, critical-thinking and analytical skills, math and problem-solving skills, excellent speaking and writing skills
>
> **Certification and Licensing**
> Not required for entry-level positions
>
> **Working Conditions**
> Indoors
>
> **Salary Range**
> About \$55,230 to \$130,930
>
> **Number of Jobs**
> About 257,900 in 2016
>
> **Future Job Outlook**
> Growth of 10 percent through 2026

When industrial engineers are faced with a problem to solve, their first step is observation. They must become thoroughly familiar with a business's day-to-day operations, such as how employees in a factory assemble automobiles or the exact procedure followed when a major retailer ships merchandise to customers. By developing familiarity with how an organization goes about its business, industrial engineers can zero in on any problems—those that exist and those that are likely to develop in the future if changes are not made. This phase often involves studying people while they work, reviewing historical data and production schedules, and taking other steps to understand the organization inside and out.

Once industrial engineers have completed the observation phase, they compile their findings into a presentation for decision makers. This meeting is where any specific recommendations for improvement are presented, such as computerized systems designed to remedy a particular problem. For example, an industrial engineer might design a system for a manufacturing operation that moves heavy parts within a factory or one that schedules workers and monitors their performance. For a large retailer, a new system might improve inventory control and streamline the ordering and shipment processes. For a health care organization, an industrial engineer might design a system that helps reduce patient wait time in emergency rooms and schedules doctors and nurses based on when need is the greatest. For a transportation and logistics company, a new system can determine how delivery trucks should be routed throughout a town or the country and whether shipments should be sent by truck, rail, or air.

The supermarket chain Publix has an industrial engineer job description on its website. The document explains that industrial engineers help improve operational efficiency at company facilities that produce bakery and other food items. These engineers analyze current manufacturing processes to determine where improvement is needed. They develop requirements for the production process, including the amount of time it should take for a product to be manufactured and the most efficient work flow. The final step is implementation: putting the new recommendations into practice and making it part of the company's manufacturing processes.

How Do You Become an Industrial Engineer?

Education

A college education is a must for industrial engineers. They need a minimum of a bachelor's degree, preferably from an engineering program accredited by the Accreditation Board for

Engineering Technology (ABET). Many major in industrial engineering, but other common focuses are general engineering, mechanical engineering, and manufacturing engineering. Course work varies based on the specialty, but industrial engineering students study statistics, economics, physics, production systems planning, manufacturing systems design, and quality control. Because their jobs will involve working with people, they also take classes in communications, psychology, sociology, and organizational behavior. According to the Bureau of Labor Statistics (BLS), several colleges and universities offer five-year degree programs in industrial engineering that lead to both a bachelor's and a master's degree.

Brianne Bujnowski is an industrial engineering student at the University of Miami College of Engineering. She has always loved math and problem solving, so an engineering career seemed like the perfect fit—or a "no-brainer," as she refers to it. Bujnowski chose to specialize in industrial engineering because, compared with many other engineering specialties, it would allow her to spend much of her time working with people. She discusses this in a December 2017 interview that appears on the Society of Women Engineers blog. "Industrial engineering is all about working with others to solve a problem and make processes more efficient," says Bujnowski. "Once I heard that, I immediately knew it was the major for me."

Certification

Once industrial engineering students have earned a bachelor's degree, no certification or licensure is required for entry-level jobs. Earning their Professional Engineering (PE) certification has numerous advantages, however, such as higher-level leadership positions and higher salary, as well as the credibility and respect that comes along with holding the PE license. "Being a licensed engineer is a big deal if you want to climb the ladder in your profession," says the educational resource group Brightwood Engineering Education in an article on its website.

Once they have earned a bachelor's degree from an ABET-accredited engineering program, students must take—and pass—the Fundamentals of Engineering exam. After working for at least four years in an engineering job under a PE-licensed engineer, they are eligible to take the PE exam. A passing score makes them eligible to be licensed as a professional engineer in their own state.

Volunteer Work and Internships

Aspiring industrial engineers can benefit from getting involved in volunteer work. By volunteering their time and talents in their communities, they can help others while strengthening their communication, project management, and team-building skills. The University of Texas–El Paso College of Engineering has a volunteer corps called the Ninjaneers. Members take part in tours for high school students, helping plan the events and serving as tour guides. Ninjaneers also serve as mentors to other engineering college students and provide tutoring services to their peers who seek academic support.

Internships can be invaluable for industrial engineering students. These usually take place during the summer months, when school is on break, and many students intern every summer during college. The type of hands-on experience they gain from internships is highly attractive to employers, who tend to choose job candidates who have work experience along with a college education. In an October 2017 interview on the Purdue University website, president Mitch Daniels touts the school's Pathmaker Internship Program. "There is no program at Purdue that I'm more excited about," says Daniels. "An internship gives students experience and exposure, but most importantly, real world practice in their chosen field of study."

Skills and Personality

Industrial engineers wear many different hats, so they need a unique combination of skills and personality traits. Excellent problem-solving skills are essential, as are critical-thinking skills. Industrial engineers must be analytical, be mathematically inclined, and have a good grasp on the principles of finance, economics, and statistics. Technical skills are a must, since industrial engineers use a variety of computer software in the course of their jobs.

Equally important for industrial engineers are communication skills, including the ability to listen well and speak (and write) clearly. They must be able to get along well with others and work effectively on teams because they will be relying on others for input and information about problems that need fixing. It is also crucial for industrial engineers to be confident when discussing problems with decision makers, as well as tactful. It can be difficult for people to accept change—and the very essence of an industrial engineer's job is recommending changes. "Few people really enjoy and embrace change, even if they know it's necessary for the business to succeed," says Brightwood Engineering Education. "So, in addition to being analytical and curious, [industrial engineers] must also be tactful and confident."

On the Job

Employers

According to the BLS, industrial engineers held nearly 258,000 jobs in the United States during 2016. The majority are employed by some type of manufacturing operation, with the highest percentage employed by transportation equipment manufacturers. These include companies that manufacture motor vehicles and motor vehicle parts, aerospace products and parts, ships and boats, and railroad rolling stock (locomotives, coaches, and railroad cars). Industrial engineers also work for manufacturers of computers and electronic parts, miscellaneous machinery, and fabricated metal products. About 13 percent work for professional, scientific, or technical service industries.

Working Conditions

The majority of industrial engineers work full time. Their hours vary based on the projects in which they are involved, as well as their particular industry. They often work in offices using computers to analyze data they have collected, design computer systems, or prepare reports for decision makers. It is also common for industrial engineers to spend time in the settings they are charged with improving. For instance, an industrial engineer who is trying to identify problems in a manufacturing operation will spend time watching employees at work in the company's factory. On the My Cool Job website, industrial and systems manufacturing engineer Tim Leopold describes this: "My typical work day has a nice balance of engineering work done behind a computer, where I will study a particular problem, with frequent trips to the manufacturing floor to go to the actual spot to determine the actual problem."

When asked how they like what they do for a living, industrial engineers typically express a high level of job satisfaction. Most find their jobs to be enjoyable and intellectually challenging, and they especially like the variety of tasks; in other words, no two days are exactly the same.

Earnings

Industrial engineers, says the BLS, were earning an average of $85,880 per year as of May 2017. These salaries ranged from a low of about $55,000 to more than $130,930, earned by the top 10 percent in the field. The industries that paid the highest wages (in the following order) were computer and electronic product manufacturing; professional, scientific, and technical services; transportation equipment manufacturing; machinery manufacturing; and fabricated metal product manufacturing.

Opportunities for Advancement

Industrial engineers who are new to their careers usually work under the supervision of experienced engineers for several years (a minimum of four years for those who seek PE licensure). As new employees gain knowledge and experience, they may advance to positions such as quality engineers or facility planners. In that role, says the BLS, they supervise teams of engineers and technicians and may eventually move into management positions. Holding a master's degree provides an edge for industrial engineers who want to attain these higher-level positions.

What Is the Future Outlook for Industrial Engineers?

The BLS projects that employment of industrial engineers will grow 10 percent through 2026, which is faster than average for all occupations. This projection means that more than twenty-five thousand new industrial engineering jobs will be created in the coming years. Industrial engineers will be needed for a wide range of industries, including consulting and engineering services, research and development firms, and manufacturing. Because industrial engineering is closely linked to manufacturing, the need for industrial engineers rises and falls based on the success (or failure) of manufacturing industries. This has always been the case and will continue to be the case in the future, which is why the projected demand for industrial engineers is 10 percent, rather than a higher number. "Projected declines in overall employment in some manufacturing sectors will temper total growth for industrial engineers," says the BLS.

Find Out More

Institute of Industrial & Systems Engineers (IISE)
3577 Parkway Lane, Suite 200
Norcross, GA 30092
website: www.iise.org

The IISE is dedicated to the support of the industrial engineering profession and individuals involved with improving quality and productivity. Its website offers a variety of publications about industrial engineering and a section called Career Center that offers good information to those who are considering industrial engineer careers.

National Society of Professional Engineers (NSPE)
1420 King St.
Alexandria, VA 22314
website: www.nspe.org

The NSPE seeks to address the professional concerns of licensed professional engineers of all disciplines and specialties. Aspiring industrial engineers will find much good information on the NSPE website, from a special Student Resources section to news articles, podcasts, a newsletter, and a search engine that produces numerous articles related to industrial engineering.

Purdue University School of Industrial Engineering
701 W. Stadium Ave.
West Lafayette, IN 47907
website: https://engineering.purdue.edu/IE

Purdue's School of Industrial Engineering has been consistently rated as one of the top industrial engineering schools in the United States. Aspiring industrial engineers will find a lot of good material on the website, including why industrial engineering is a good career choice, research areas, interviews with industrial engineering graduates, and links to the archived *ReThink IE* online magazine.

Sloan Career Cornerstone Center—Industrial Engineering
website: www.careercornerstone.org

The Sloan Career Cornerstone Center is an online resource that provides information on careers in science, technology, engineering, and more. The website offers guidance on more than 185 degree fields, including industrial engineering. Site visitors will learn about what it is like to work as an industrial engineer, preparing for a career as an industrial engineer, future employment projections, and more.

Environmental Engineer

What Does an Environmental Engineer Do?

Environmental engineers work to protect the planet and keep its inhabitants safe. They are responsible for coming up with solutions to environmental problems, such as polluted soil, air, or water. At the heart of an environmental engineer's job is sustainability, which is the concept of using natural resources to meet today's needs without compromising the environment for future generations.

> **At a Glance**
>
> **Environmental Engineer**
>
> **Minimum Educational Requirements**
> Bachelor's degree
>
> **Personal Qualities**
> Imagination and creativity, problem-solving skills, reading and writing skills, interpersonal skills
>
> **Certification and Licensing**
> Not required for entry-level positions
>
> **Working Conditions**
> Variety of indoor and outdoor locations
>
> **Salary Range**
> About $52,160 to more than $134,060
>
> **Number of Jobs**
> About 53,800 in 2016
>
> **Future Job Outlook**
> Growth of 8 percent through 2026

Those who work in environmental engineering are involved in a variety of projects, often managing several projects at once. They may study the effects of acid rain on a forest, damage to the ozone layer from airborne pollutants, or smog from automobile emissions. One environmental engineer might focus on unsafe drinking water, such as water that has been found to contain high amounts of lead, while another's focus is on climate change and what it could mean for the planet and human health in both the short and long term. Environmental engineers study and design systems for municipal and industrial water supplies and industrial wastewater. They coordinate solid waste management and recycling activities for municipalities and industry. They also study the environmental impact of proposed development projects long before construction begins.

The specific tasks performed by environmental engineers vary based on their projects. After conducting an investigation, for instance, they prepare reports and keep them current through regular updates. Environmental engineers counsel corporations and government agencies about the best ways to clean up contaminated sites. They analyze scientific data and conduct quality control checks whenever necessary. They monitor the progress of environmental improvement programs and inspect industrial and municipal facilities to ensure they are compliant with environmental regulations—which is a crucial part of their job. As environmental engineer Dan Wittliff explains in a 2017 *U.S. News & World Report* article, "In terms of what an environmental engineer does day in and day out, you're really focused on what the regulations say, what you're required to do to meet those regulations and how you're going to do it."

Danny Yodzis is an environmental engineer who works for an environmental consulting firm in Columbus, Ohio. He designs green infrastructure projects, meaning better ways of managing stormwater runoff, which is a major source of pollution in urban areas. For Yodzis, this involves designing sanitary sewers and pump stations, as well as treatment plants for water and wastewater. For every one of his projects, he is responsible for performing preliminary studies, writing technical memos and design reports, designing detailed plans, and providing construction management services.

How Do You Become an Environmental Engineer?

Education

The minimum educational requirement for an environmental engineer is a bachelor's degree. Those who are interested in earning their Professional Engineering (PE) certification later in their career should attend a college or university whose engineering program has been accredited by the Accreditation Board for Engineering Technology. Many environmental engineers hold degrees in environmental engineering, although some choose another specialty, such as civil engineering, chemical engineering, or general engineering.

While attending college, students will work in the classroom, in the laboratory, and also out in the field conducting experiments and taking various kinds of measurements, such as emissions from building materials or water suspected of being contaminated by agricultural runoff. Classroom course work is heavy on science and math, including calculus, physics, chemistry, environmental science, and biology. To prepare for this tough college load, education advisers encourage aspiring environmental engineers to choose high school curricula that include chemistry, biology, physics, and math courses, including algebra, geometry, trigonometry, and calculus.

Certification

Environmental engineers who are just getting started in their careers do not need to be licensed. Later, however, PE certification is highly recommended, and many employers require their engineers to be licensed. The first step toward becoming a licensed PE is for students to take the Fundamentals of Engineering exam and earn a passing score. They must work for a minimum of four years under a licensed engineer and then pass the PE exam. Each state has its own licensing board and procedures for issuing PE licenses to qualifying engineers.

After earning their PE license, environmental engineers may work toward further certification through the American Academy of Environmental Engineers and Scientists (AAEES). This certification carries a high level of distinction, and requirements are rigorous. In addition to the four years of work experience required for the PE license, environmental engineers must accumulate four more years of full-time environmental engineering experience, as well as pass written and oral examinations. They must also be known for their professionalism, integrity, and good moral character. If these criteria are met, the AAEES board of trustees may grant a candidate the designation of Board Certified Environmental Engineer.

Volunteer Work and Internships

Aspiring environmental engineers can become involved in volunteer endeavors that enhance their knowledge and provide them with experience. At engineering summer camps, for example, young people learn about what engineers actually do and get ideas for planning their high school curriculum. One example is the Environmental and Sustainable Engineering summer camp that is held at the University of Illinois at Urbana-Champaign in Champaign, Illinois. Students who attend the camp participate in a variety of activities that focus on issues such as climate change, renewable energy (solar, wind, and tidal), and water, including the various factors that can affect water quality.

Aspiring engineers can also volunteer with environmental organizations in their communities or join engineering student groups. In a 2017 "Environmental Engineering Success Stories" article on the Ohio State University website, environmental engineer Michael Irwin touts the value of student groups: "Some of the most valuable things these student groups provide is the opportunity to attend professional panels (hear experiences from engineers, great networking opportunity) and facility tours (get a chance to see and become familiar with the actual treatment plants, landfills, and remediation sites that environmental engineers design)."

Internships are a must for aspiring environmental engineers. Most are paid positions and usually take place during the summer, when college students are on break. By interning, young people can gain hands-on work experience in their chosen career field, which employers value highly when considering applicants for jobs. Another benefit of internships is they help young people make decisions about what jobs interest them and what jobs do not interest them. Columbus, Ohio, environmental engineer Jon Miner explains in the 2017 "Environmental Engineering Success Stories" article, "You may find that there are certain fields in engineering that you do not particularly like and it is much better to find that out in an internship setting than it is to find out once you're in a full time position."

Skills and Personality

A number of skills and personality traits are important for young people who want to pursue careers in environmental engineering. Problem-solving skills are a must, since an environmental engineer's job revolves around solving problems from safeguarding workers' health to figuring out ways to prevent environmental damage when new construction is planned. Creativity and imagination go hand in hand with problem-solving skills. Being comfortable with technology is essential because environmental engineers use a variety of computer software in their jobs, and software changes constantly.

Another must for environmental engineers is excellent communication skills, including speaking, listening, and writing. They need to be able to get along with people, work effectively in teams, and have a good attitude. Also essential is not getting frustrated when unplanned (and unwelcome) changes occur, because according to people who work in environmental engineering, continuous change is a given.

On the Job

Employers

According to the Bureau of Labor Statistics (BLS), environmental engineers held nearly fifty-four thousand jobs in 2016. The largest employers were engineering service firms, closely followed by management, scientific, and technical consulting services. The third-largest employer of environmental engineers is state governments, followed by local and federal governments. In a November 2016 *Berkeley Science Review* article, environmental engineering PhD student Emily Cook describes the diverse industries that employ environmental engineers: "You could work for city utilities on water treatment and quality or a consulting firm to design new water treatment plants. You could do research fulltime . . . or you

Environmental engineers inspect industrial and municipal facilities to make sure they comply with environmental laws. By analyzing data, they can determine progress on environmental improvement programs.

could work in government or on policy for such entities as the US Environmental Protection Agency (EPA) and the Department of Energy (DOE). The field is incredibly diverse—and its diversity is only continuing to increase."

Working Conditions

Most environmental engineers work full time, and those with heavy project loads often work more than forty hours per week. According to the AAEES, working longer hours is just part of the job, as explained on the group's website. "If you take up a job as an environmental engineer, expect to work over 40 hours per week."

Environmental engineers work in different types of locations depending on the nature of their tasks. If they meet with urban and regional planners, scientists, or other professionals, these meetings typically take place in an office setting. Writing plans or reports, or designing projects on a computer, are also office activities. When overseeing construction, sampling groundwater, or examining environmental damage from contamination, environmental engineers work outdoors at job sites.

In terms of job satisfaction, environmental engineers typically report being happy with their chosen careers. On its website, the AAEES acknowledges that environmental engineering is not a glamorous job, but it benefits the planet and society. "Knowing that you are helping society every day can offer plenty of job satisfaction," says the AAEES.

Earnings

Environmental engineering is a career that offers higher-than-average pay. According to the BLS, as of May 2017 environmental engineers' annual salary averaged $86,800. The lowest-paid 10 percent earned about $52,000, and the highest-paid 10 percent earned more than $134,000.

The industries that paid the highest annual wages were (in the following order): the federal government; some local government agencies; engineering service firms; management, scientific, and technical consulting services; and some state government agencies.

Opportunities for Advancement

Like all engineers, environmental engineers must pay their dues before their careers can take off. Over the years, as they gain knowledge and experience and prove themselves to be capable and dependable, they may move on to more difficult and challenging projects. Those who are licensed and become board certified by the AAEES have the best chance of being promoted to higher-level positions, such as engineering managers or program managers.

What Is the Future Outlook for Environmental Engineers?

The future looks promising for environmental engineers. According to the BLS, environmental engineering jobs will grow by 8 percent through 2026, which is slightly faster than the average for all occupations. That amounts to forty-five hundred new jobs for environmental engineers.

Most of the projected employment growth for environmental engineers, says the BLS, will be in professional, scientific, and technical service organizations. As state and local governments grow more concerned about water and more efficient water use, they will turn to these entities for assistance. Environmental engineers will also be needed to address the federal government's requirement for contaminated site cleanup and to help utility companies and water-treatment plants comply with federal and state environmental regulations.

Find Out More

American Academy of Environmental Engineers (AAEE)
121 Madison Ave.
New York, NY 92103
website: www.aaee.net

The AAEE is devoted to educating people about the field of environmental engineering. Its website offers plenty of information for aspiring engineers, covering topics such as why the career is worth pursuing, a day in the life of an environmental engineer, what companies look for when hiring environmental engineers, and many more topics of interest.

American Academy of Environmental Engineers and Scientists (AAEES)
147 Old Solomons Island Rd., Suite 303
Annapolis, MD 21401
website: www.aaees.org

The AAEES serves the environmental engineering and environmental science professions by providing board certification to those who qualify through experience and testing. The AAEES website offers a number of environmental publications, information on environmental engineering careers, and a Student Resources section.

Engineers Without Borders

1031 Thirty-Third St., Suite 210
Denver, CO 80205
website: www.ewb-usa.org

With 16,800 members, Engineers Without Borders seeks to build a better world through engineering projects that help people and communities in developing countries. Its website offers numerous articles about how environmental engineers are volunteering their time to make these projects possible, and also links to a blog with more information.

University of Michigan Department of Civil & Environmental Engineering

2350 Hayward St.
2105 GG Brown Building
Ann Arbor, MI 48109
website: http://cee.engin.umich.edu
Founded in 1837, the University of Michigan Department of Civil & Environmental Engineering has been ranked as one of the best college engineering programs in the United States. The department's website offers many informative research articles about how civil and environmental engineering are addressing problems throughout the nation.

Mechanical Engineer

What Does a Mechanical Engineer Do?

Mechanical engineers create the machines and devices that enable society to function. These may range from small and simple (pens, pencils, bicycle chains, and screwdrivers) to large and complex (internal combustion engines, GPS satellites, and robots used in a factory). It is the job of mechanical engineers to research, design, construct, and test machines and devices of every conceivable shape and size. They also create the machines that build those objects, as well as the processes that are necessary to manufacture them. "Pretty much any machine or process you can think of has been touched by a mechanical engineer at some point," says Brightwood Engineering Education in an August 2017 article on its website.

At a Glance

Mechanical Engineer

Minimum Educational Requirements
Bachelor's degree

Personal Qualities
Problem-solving and analytic skills, math skills, communication skills, good interpersonal skills

Certification and Licensing
Not required for entry-level positions

Working Conditions
Usually indoors; occasional visits to outdoor work sites

Salary Range
About $55,310 to $134,000

Number of Jobs
About 288,800 in 2016

Future Job Outlook
Growth of 9 percent through 2026

The specific tasks assigned to mechanical engineers can vary widely based on their individual projects. They might, for example, be tasked with creating a thermal sensor, which is a device that detects temperature changes in laptop and desktop computers. Mechanical engineers use computer-aided design (CAD) software to design the sensor. They build a prototype to match their design specs and then test the prototype for functionality and to identify any problems. Using a computer, they analyze the results and make any necessary modifications. When the device is ready for production, a mechanical engineer will oversee the manufacturing process.

A large number of mechanical engineers work in the automobile industry. According to the data analysis website Data USA, the auto industry alone employs more than seventy-eight thousand mechanical engineers. These professionals are involved in the design and manufacture of not only automobile engines but a mind-boggling number of other parts. In a June 2017 *Forbes* article, mechanical engineer Betsy Megas writes, "I'm sure you've seen a car, but have you ever really looked at one? There's a ton of stuff in it. . . . Somebody—in fact lots of somebodies—have to design, analyze, and test all that stuff." Megas describes some of this "stuff," including seats, seat belts, airbags, windshield wipers, shock absorbers, plastic taillight covers, a ventilation system, and a frame that is specially designed to crumple in the event of a crash in order to dissipate energy. The various parts of a vehicle, as well as the machinery that builds them, were all developed by mechanical engineers.

Mechanical engineers often choose to specialize in a particular area. One of these is auto research, which seeks to improve traditional features of automobiles, such as suspension systems and fuel systems. Another specialization is heating and cooling. Mechanical engineers who choose this specialty create and maintain environmental systems where there is a need for temperature and humidity to be kept within certain limits. These systems, says the Bureau of Labor Statistics (BLS), may be developed for transportation, such as airplanes, trains, and automobiles, as well as for schools and computer rooms located inside buildings.

One mechanical engineering specialty that is growing more popular—and more in demand—is robotics. Mechanical engineers who specialize in this area conceive, design, build, and maintain robots and robotic systems. Matthew Brady is a mechanical engineer who works for Amazon Robotics, a subsidiary of Amazon that manufactures robotic systems. His job involves new product development for Amazon's fulfillment center robots, as well as working to maintain and support existing robotics equipment. "This entails doing mechanical design for new concepts, designing and building prototypes, and completing long-term durability testing," Brady explains in a 2017 "Environmental Engineering Success Stories" article on the Ohio State University website.

How Do You Become a Mechanical Engineer?

Education

A career in mechanical engineering requires a minimum of a bachelor's degree, usually in mechanical engineering or mechanical engineering technology. Those who plan to become licensed later in their careers should attend a school whose engineering program has been accredited by the Accreditation Board for Engineering Technology. These students' college curriculum is typically heavy in mathematics (calculus, statistics, and trigonometry) and sciences (chemistry, physics, and molecular biology), and it also includes classes in mechanical design, engineering design, computer programming, and CAD, among a variety of others.

Many aspiring mechanical engineers go beyond their bachelor's degree to earn a master's degree. Education advisers say graduate degrees are becoming more important because they provide students with opportunities to develop a specialization and have a more concentrated engineering experience. This was the case with Brady, who enrolled in a master's degree program immediately after finishing his bachelor's degree at the University of Pennsylvania in 2015. He selected course work that was heavily focused on robotics, which led to his job at Amazon Robotics. According to the BLS, some colleges and universities offer five-year programs that enable students to earn both a bachelor's and a master's degree.

A mechanical engineer uses a computer-aided design program to develop a prototype of a new device. Many mechanical engineers are involved in the design and manufacture of car parts, while others work in robotics or other fields.

Certification

Licensure is not required for entry-level mechanical engineer positions, but earning the Professional Engineering (PE) certification is highly recommended. Once aspiring mechanical engineers earn a bachelor's degree from an accredited engineering program, there are three steps they must follow to be licensed and certified as a PE: pass the Fundamentals of Engineering exam, work for four years under a licensed professional engineer, and earn a passing score on the PE exam. Mechanical engineers who have completed all the necessary qualifications are licensed by the state in which they live.

Additional certifications are available for mechanical engineers who are interested. Along with being certified by the American Society of Mechanical Engineers, several other specialty organizations offer their own certification programs. These include the National Fire Prevention Association, Association for Facilities Engineering, Project Management Institute, Engineering Management Certification International, and Green Building Certification

Institute. Although not everyone chooses to earn these certifications, licensed mechanical engineers with one or more certifications often have an edge over those who do not.

Volunteer Work and Internships

Volunteer opportunities abound for aspiring mechanical engineers. An especially popular and valuable activity is involvement with student engineering groups. Mechanical engineer Derek Riddle highly recommends that young people join student groups. While attending Ohio State University, Riddle was involved with the college of engineering's Formula Buckeyes team. Its name comes from Ohio State's official nickname (Buckeyes) and the group's chief endeavor: giving engineering students opportunities to learn from designing, building, testing, developing, and racing a formula-style race car. In the 2017 Ohio State University "Environmental Engineering Success Stories" article, Riddle explains the value of being involved with the Formula Buckeyes group: "The knowledge I gained there allowed me to meet people, identify what I wanted to do in my career, and gave me the real engineering experience that I credit with most of the opportunities I have gotten in industry so far."

Career experts and educator advisers stress the importance of internships for aspiring mechanical engineers. These are typically paid positions and often take place during the summer months, when students are on break from school. Closely related to internships are co-op programs, in which students work at a job in their chosen field during the school year. The benefits are twofold: They gain valuable real-world experience and earn money to help finance their college education. An added benefit to both internships and co-op programs is that students have a good chance of being hired by the companies for whom they have been working.

Skills and Personality

Mechanical engineers need many different skills in order to succeed in their careers, with problem-solving skills of the utmost importance. They must be analytical and able to think creatively because problem solving requires creative solutions. They need to be mathematically inclined and have good technical skills, as well as the ability to multitask, since they will undoubtedly work on several projects at once. Closely related to multitasking is the ability to work well under pressure without becoming flustered.

Personality traits needed by mechanical engineers include good interpersonal skills and the ability to work effectively in teams. Good communication skills (listening as well as talking) are essential, as is the ability to write well and get concepts and ideas across. "Creating a product is only part of the equation," a representative of Michigan Technological University explains on the school's website. "Knowing how to work with people, ideas, data, and economics fully makes a mechanical engineer."

On the Job

Employers

According to the BLS, mechanical engineers held about 288,800 jobs during 2016. The largest employers that year were private companies, such as architectural, engineering, and other types of related service firms. The second-largest employers of mechanical engineers were machinery manufacturers, with nearly as many employed by transportation equipment manufacturers. Other top employers included scientific research and development service firms and computer and electronic product manufacturing firms.

Working Conditions

Most mechanical engineers work full time, with an estimated three out of ten working more than forty hours per week. They spend much of their time working inside, either in offices using computers or at other facilities, such as warehouses, fulfillment centers, or manufacturing plants, wherever their work happens to be. Mechanical engineer Steve Blumenkranz writes on the knowledge-sharing platform Quora that people in his profession typically spend most of their time in an office. "However," he says, "we leave our seats to go to the laboratory, the machine shop, the manufacturing area, the receiving dock, for lunch and to take a healthful walk."

Some mechanical engineering jobs involve a lot of travel. In her job as a mechanical engineer with Caterpillar Inc., Sarita Kuppili designs track chains for the undercarriages of excavators and tractors. Her work has taken her to China, Korea, Japan, India, Italy, and France. "The machines we design help build infrastructure, mining, support disaster relief, and protect environment projects around the world," says Kuppili in an August 2017 article on the Society of Women Engineers blog.

Earnings

Mechanical engineering is a career that pays very well. According to the BLS, mechanical engineers earned an average of $85,880 per year as of May 2017. Wages for the lowest-paid 10 percent were about $55,310 per year, and the highest-paid 10 percent earned more than $133,900.

The highest-paying industry for mechanical engineers was (collectively) scientific, research, and development service firms, which paid more than $98,500 per year. Other industries that paid the best wages include (from highest to lowest) computer and electronic product manufacturing; architectural, engineering, and related service firms; transportation equipment manufacturers; and machinery manufacturers.

Opportunities for Advancement

Mechanical engineers typically need to work for a number of years to establish themselves before moving up the career ladder. After gaining work experience and earning their PE certification, mechanical engineers may be promoted to senior-level engineer positions or upper-level management positions. Those who are interested in high-level research and development programs or teaching at the university level need to continue their education and earn a PhD.

What Is the Future Outlook for Mechanical Engineers?

Mechanical engineers are in high demand, and labor experts see that trend continuing in the future. The BLS predicts that employment of mechanical engineers will grow by 9 percent through 2026, which is slightly faster than the 7 percent average for all occupations. This percentage translates to 25,300 new mechanical engineering jobs in the not-too-distant future. The fields that will offer the greatest potential for aspiring mechanical engineers include robotics, alternative energies, and nanotechnology, which involves manipulating matter at the tiniest levels, such as atoms and molecules.

Find Out More

American Society of Mechanical Engineers (ASME)
2 Park Ave.
New York, NY 10016
website: www.asme.org

The ASME focuses on technical, educational, and research issues of interest to the engineering and technology community. Its website's Topics section offers numerous publications covering careers in mechanical engineering and technical issues, such as robotics, manufacturing, energy, and 3D printing.

Bureau of Labor Statistics (BLS)
Office of Occupational Statistics and Employment Projections
PSB Suite 2135, 2 Massachusetts Ave. NE
Washington, DC 20212
website: www.bls.gov

The BLS is the United States's chief statistical agency responsible for measuring labor market activity, working conditions, and price changes in the economy. The *Occupational Outlook Hand-*

book, found on the BLS website, offers a wealth of information about engineering jobs, including mechanical engineers and mechanical engineer technicians.

Institution of Mechanical Engineers

1 Birdcage Walk
London
SW1H9JJ
United Kingdom
website: www.imeche.org

The Institution of Mechanical Engineers, which has members in 140 countries, is an independent professional association that represents mechanical engineers and the engineering profession. Its website offers information about the various industries served by mechanical engineers, education and training, current industry news, and a library of digital resources.

Society of Automotive Engineers

400 Commonwealth Dr.
Warrendale, PA 15096
website: www.sae.org

The Society of Automotive Engineers is made up of more than 128,000 engineers and related technical experts in the aerospace, automotive, and commercial-vehicle industries. Its website offers a great deal of information of interest to aspiring mechanical engineers, including magazines, journals, and technical papers, as well as current news, videos, and webcasts.

Electrical Engineer

What Does an Electrical Engineer Do?

Electrical engineers are problem solvers and builders of electrical equipment and electronics. From electric motors to radar, power generation equipment, aircraft, computer chips, and ultra-tiny smartphone circuit boards, electrical engineers design, develop, implement, and improve the products that keep society humming. "In today's technology driven world, electrical engineering is the cornerstone and driver of innovation of the devices we utilize daily to improve our quality of life," the New Jersey Institute of Technology states on its website.

As they go about their jobs, electrical engineers perform a wide variety of tasks. They may develop new electrical systems from beginning to end. They spend time troubleshooting when electrical systems or processes do not work the way they are supposed to. When complaints from customers or the public need investigating, electrical engineers take care of that as well, and then recommend solutions to problems that have been identified. They also spend quite a bit of time attending meet-

At a Glance

Electrical Engineer

Minimum Educational Requirements
Bachelor's degree

Personal Qualities
Math skills, good speaking and writing skills, ability to concentrate and focus on the job, interpersonal skills

Certification and Licensing
Not required for entry-level positions

Working Conditions
Usually indoors; occasional visits to outdoor work sites

Salary Range
About $60,250 to more than $150,000 per year

Number of Jobs
About 188,300 in 2016

Future Job Outlook
Growth of 9 percent through 2026

ings with project managers, architects, and draftspersons, as well as with clients for whom they are designing electrical projects.

When electrical engineers have been tasked with creating something new, they are responsible for every step of product development. Although their specific duties will differ based on what they are developing, the process they follow is basically the same from project to project. The first step is to identify a need or problem: Why is a new electrical device or system desired, and what will it do? Once this information has been determined, the electrical engineer can begin work on initial designs, which are typically created on a computer using sophisticated design or modeling software.

After the designs are finished, the electrical engineer creates a prototype of the device. This is an important part of the process, since it can reveal any flaws or areas needing improvement or tweaking. "The prototype serves as a validation of the original idea," says Brightwood Engineering Education in an August 2017 article on its website. "It can also function as a test to determine whether the initial idea will result in a product that can be designed for manufacturability." Once any prototype issues have been addressed, the device is ready for manufacturing. Electrical engineers oversee manufacture, implementation, and testing to ensure that the device meets all applicable specifications and codes.

One highly sophisticated piece of equipment in which electrical engineers play an essential role is a satellite. There are nearly five thousand satellites orbiting the earth, about half of which were operational as of 2018. These include GPS and other navigational satellites; weather satellites; astronomical satellites, which transmit information about outer space to ground research stations; and communications satellites, which provide customers in certain regions in the world with television, telephone, and Internet service. Electrical engineers who specialize in satellites (often called satellite engineers) design command systems that direct orbiting satellites. These systems allow satellites to be remotely controlled from ground stations. Electrical engineers are also responsible for collecting and analyzing data that has been transmitted by satellites, as well as monitoring them as they orbit.

Fiona Redmond is an electrical engineer with Hughes Network Systems, a satellite Internet provider located in Maryland. In her role as a satellite and capacity engineer, she monitors Hughes's satellites while they are in orbit. She also manages the satellites' bandwidth, which is the amount of data that is transmitted in a given period of time. In a May 2018 article on the Society of Women Engineers blog, Redmond discusses her job: "Some days I'm writing code to analyze data we collect from the satellites; other days I'm planning out where we will allocate bandwidth and planning possible changes to improve our customer experience." An exciting event that she participated in was her company's launch of its latest satellite, *Jupiter 2*. "As the satellite was brought into orbit," says Redmond, "we analyzed the data to make sure all the components were working as expected before bringing our service up on it." Like most electrical engineers, Redmond's job holds a great deal of variety. "Every day is different," she says.

How Do You Become an Electrical Engineer?

Education

A career in electrical engineering requires a bachelor's degree from a college or university whose engineering program has been accredited by the Accreditation Board for Engineering Technology (ABET). Most aspiring electrical engineers earn their degree in electrical engineering, although other popular specialties include electronics engineering and electrical engineering technology. Engineering programs feature laboratory work and fieldwork, as well as rigorous classroom course work. Curricula will vary based on the school but typically include classes such as physics and advanced physics, chemistry, calculus, linear algebra, and circuits and systems design. Other classes are computer science, digital signal processing, electrical circuit theory, and electromagnetic theory. The Bureau of Labor Statistics (BLS) says that young people who plan to major in engineering in college would benefit from taking high school classes in physics, algebra, trigonometry, and calculus. Drafting classes are also recommended because electrical engineers often rely on drafting skills to prepare technical drawings.

Also according to the BLS, some universities offer five-year programs that allow students to earn both a bachelor's and master's degree. Although graduate degrees are not required for electrical engineers, advanced education can open the door to higher-level responsibilities, leadership positions, and higher earnings.

Certification

Licensure is not required for entry-level electrical engineering positions, but earning the Professional Engineering (PE) certification at some point is nearly always required. Once students have earned a bachelor's degree from a school whose engineering program has been ABET accredited, there are three steps toward being certified as a PE: pass the Fundamentals of Engineering exam, work for a minimum of four years under a licensed professional engineer, and earn a passing score on the PE exam. Once electrical engineers have completed all the necessary qualifications, they can apply for licensing in the state in which they live.

Volunteer Work and Internships

Aspiring electrical engineers can choose to volunteer in many different ways. They can, for instance, attend engineering summer camps to see what the various types of engineers do in their jobs. Another benefit of attending these camps, says the BLS, is that aspiring engineers can get ideas for tailoring their course work for the remainder of their high school years.

Involvement in clubs and student groups is another great volunteer experience for aspiring electrical engineers. When Redmond was attending the University of Maryland, she was involved in a variety of groups, one of which was the Flexus Women in Engineering Living & Learning Community. The program was designed to help young women connect with their fellow female engineering students and provide encouragement to each other. "It was a great way to build a support system and find friends to study with," Redmond says.

Career experts and education advisers strongly advise electrical engineering students to participate in internships. These real-life work experiences, which typically take place during the summer when school is on break, can be invaluable to young people who learn firsthand what electrical engineers do. Later, those who are job hunting have a much better chance of being hired for entry-level electrical engineering positions if they have had on-the-job experience in their chosen field.

Skills and Personality

A number of skills are essential for those who work as electrical engineers. One is being mathematically inclined and able to apply the principles of calculus and other advanced math while they work. Communication skills (listening and speaking) are important because electrical engineers must be able to interact with others and explain the reasoning behind their concepts and designs. They also need good concentration skills and good time-management skills.

One important personality trait needed by electrical engineers is good interpersonal skills. They must be able to get along well with other people, since they will interact with coworkers, clients, and the public. Other important traits include being a team player and being open minded and willing to consider other points of view.

On the Job

Employers

In 2016 electrical engineers in the United States held more than 188,000 jobs. The largest employers of electrical engineers were engineering service firms, followed by electric power generation, transmission, and distribution operations. Other large employers of electrical engineers include research and development firms that focus on the physical, engineering, and life sciences; semiconductor and other electronic component manufacturers; and factories that manufacture navigational, measuring, electromedical, and control instruments (in that order).

Working Conditions

Most electrical engineers work full time and often work more than forty hours per week if a particularly challenging project requires it. They generally work indoors in offices, although they may visit work sites to attend meetings, perform inspections to ensure that electrical systems are in compliance with standards and electrical code, or perform ongoing maintenance.

As for job satisfaction, electrical engineers typically enjoy what they do for a living. In a 2014 YouTube video, John Poots, an electrical engineer for Intel, describes himself as a person "who gets bored very easily." So, he says, to be able to work in a career "that changes and keeps you interested for years to come . . . is perfect."

Earnings

Electrical engineers are paid very well. The average annual wage, says the BLS, was $95,060 as of May 2017. The lowest-paid 10 percent of electrical engineers earned about $60,000 per year, while the highest-paid 10 percent earned more than $150,000.

As of May 2017 the industry that paid the highest wages to electrical engineer employees was research and development firms in the physical, engineering, and life sciences. These firms comprise a vast array of industries, including agriculture, electronics, computers, chemistry, food, geology, health, medicine, nanotechnology, oceanography, and physics, as well as many others. Another industry that pays some of the highest wages is semiconductor and other electronic component manufacturers. Other well-paying industries that hire electrical engineers include navigational, measuring, electromedical, and control instruments manufacturers; electric power generation, transmission, and distribution; and engineering service firms (in that order).

Opportunities for Advancement

Once electrical engineers have worked at a job for four or five years and earned their PE license, they have probably established themselves in their careers. They may advance to supervisory positions, in which they lead a team of engineers and technicians, or move into higher management positions. Those with outgoing personalities may be interested in moving into sales engineer positions, which can be especially lucrative for those who have a talent for working closely with customers.

What Is the Future Outlook for Electrical Engineers?

Engineering is among the hottest careers today, and electrical engineers are going to be even more in demand in the coming years. The BLS projects that employment of electrical engineers will grow 9 percent through 2026, which is faster than the average for all occupations, including the 7 percent average growth projected for engineering. This 9 percent growth amounts to more than sixteen thousand new jobs that will be available to electrical engineers through 2026. Much of the growth in electrical engineering jobs will be in new development of solar panels, semiconductors, and communications technologies. "The need to upgrade the nation's power grids will also create demand for electrical engineering services," the BLS notes on its website.

Find Out More

Cornell University, School of Electrical and Computer Engineering
Phillips Hall, Room 229
Ithaca, NY 14853
website: www.ece.cornell.edu/ece

Established in 1883, Cornell's School of Electrical and Computer Engineering was the first college electrical engineering program in the world. Its website offers a large collection of research publications, information about electrical engineering careers, details about the school's undergraduate and graduate programs, and archived news articles.

Electrical Engineering Portal

website: https://electrical-engineering-portal.com

The Electrical Engineering Portal is a valuable resource for anyone who is interested in an electrical engineering career. The website offers a variety of articles on electrical engineering, explanations of various theories, high-quality engineering literature, research papers, and even a collection of downloadable software.

Institute of Electrical and Electronics Engineers (IEEE)

3 Park Ave., 17th Floor
New York, NY 10016
website: www.ieee.org

The IEEE is a professional organization that is dedicated to advancing technology for the benefit of humanity. Its website offers many news articles, a special section for students, and a searchable database of publications about electrical engineering.

Institution of Engineering and Technology

Michael Faraday House
Six Hills Way
Stevenage
Herts
SG1 2AY
United Kingdom
website: www.theiet.org

The Institution of Engineering and Technology is one of the world's largest engineering associations. Its website offers a wide variety of publications and journals, as well as news releases and a search engine that produces numerous articles about electrical engineering.

Cartographer

What Does a Cartographer Do?

Cartographers, who are sometimes called cartographic engineers, are professional mapmakers: people who use a combination of art, science, and technology to create maps. Although paper maps, atlases, and globes are by no means obsolete and are still in use throughout the world today, maps are now created in an amazing array of shapes, sizes, and types, and they serve many purposes. From the way data is collected and analyzed to the ways maps are used in the twenty-first century, technology has transformed mapmaking. In a 2016 issue of *Library of Congress Magazine*, geography and cartography expert Ralph Ehrenberg writes, "In today's interconnected world of communications and social networking, maps are more relevant and important than ever. Whether searching for the closest convenience store, navigating a mountain trail or planning a foreign adventure, up-to-date, detailed interactive maps of every place on the Earth are immediately available through mobile devices." Even as mapmaking has changed dramatically in recent years, the cartogra-

At a Glance

Cartographer

Minimum Educational Requirements
Bachelor's degree

Personal Qualities
Computer skills, critical-thinking and decision-making skills, problem-solving skills, detail oriented

Certification and Licensing
Requirements vary by state

Working Conditions
Mostly indoors, with some outdoor fieldwork required

Salary Range
About $40,390 to more than $100,000 per year

Number of Jobs
About 12,600 in 2016

Future Job Outlook
Growth of 19 percent through 2026

phy profession has changed with it—and the demand for cartographers continues to grow.

To create maps, cartographers collect and analyze information from a variety of sources. These include (but are not limited to) existing maps; remote-sensing devices, such as satellites and aerial cameras; statistical reports; and computerized data files. One example of a remote-sensing device is a satellite. Hundreds of active orbiting satellites are continuously mapping the planet, collecting a staggering array of data and transmitting it back to receiving units on earth. Information is also gathered in other ways, such as geodetic surveys. These surveys of large areas of land have had corrections made for the curvature of the earth's surface.

Cartographers take part in most every step of the mapmaking process. They are often involved in researching and gathering information, deciding what should (and should not) appear on a map, and the best way to present the information. According to Ehrenberg, cartographers have many choices to make before they start designing a map. For example, they must determine the best way for the round earth to be depicted on a flat page or screen, which is known as map projection; how much area the map should cover, which is the scale; what colors and shapes (or symbols) should appear on the map; and how it will be printed or displayed. "Fortunately," says Ehrenberg, "with computers, cartographers can now try out a bunch of map design choices—not so long ago, each change was really time-consuming and expensive."

When it is time to create their maps, cartographers work with highly sophisticated computer software. Some of the most commonly used are digital image processing systems, computer-aided design, and geographic information system (GIS) software. Depending on where they work and what their specialty is, cartographers may use this software to create a variety of different maps. These include globes, atlases, maritime charts, statistical maps, street maps, and maps for specific purposes, such as to help tourists find their way around unfamiliar cities. Other types of specialties are topographical maps, which show the earth's natural and artificial surface features and land use; maps used for city planning, weather forecasting, or geological exploration; or maps used by the military. Digital maps, which are designed to be seen and used on a computer monitor, tablet, or smartphone, account for a fast-growing proportion of all maps made.

One type of specialty map cartographers create is the thematic map, which emphasizes a particular theme or topic. Thematic maps could show the average distribution of rainfall in a region, areas of the country with the worst poverty rates, the highest-crime cities, or political affiliations, such as cities and states that typically vote Republican (shown in red) versus Democratic (shown in blue).

One cartographer who works for the CIA creates thematic maps, which he refers to as "maps that tell a story." He does not usually take part in information gathering; most data collection is done by analysts with whom the CIA collaborates. Once he has the data, along with any other intelligence information he has gathered, he is ready to begin building his map. The thematic maps he creates may be used by CIA agents, lawmakers, military personnel in war zones, or others who need to know specific information, such as where particular events are taking place or identified risks to the United States. For this cartographer, what he does is the ideal job, as he explains in a November 2017 interview on the CIA website: "I love the satisfaction that comes with knowing my skills—combined with those of so many other talented individuals—are utilized to help inform policy and protect our country from threats abroad."

How Do You Become a Cartographer?

Education

Cartographers usually have a bachelor's degree in cartography, geography, surveying, civil engineering, or another similar field. The courses they study in college will vary depending on the major they choose but will likely include GIS technology, geography, earth science, surveying, computer programming, computer mapping, and various types of math. According to the Bureau of Labor Statistics (BLS), aspiring cartographers also need to master web-based mapping technologies, including newer types that incorporate the GPS capabilities of mobile phones and in-car navigation systems.

Graduate degrees are not required for cartographers but can prove to be an asset to one's career. According to a November 2017 article in the online technology magazine *Wired*, between 2007 and 2015, the number of college graduates who went on to earn master's degrees in cartography increased by more than 40 percent.

Certification

Cartographers are not required to be licensed when hired for entry-level positions. Licensing requirements for later in a cartographer's career vary by state. According to the BLS, some states require cartographers to be licensed as surveyors, or professionals who make precise measurements to determine property boundaries for engineering, mapmaking, and construction projects. Although licensing requirements are different from state to state, all candidates must meet educational requirements and pass a test before being licensed.

Cartographers can also benefit from being certified by the American Society for Photogrammetry and Remote Sensing or the United States Geospatial Intelligence Foundation. The BLS states that candidates must meet experience and education requirements and must pass an examination. By being certified by one or both of these organizations, cartographers are demonstrating competence and dedication to their field, and this may increase their appeal to potential employers.

Volunteer Work and Internships

Aspiring cartographers can benefit from becoming involved with organizations such as the North American Cartographic Information Society, which has student groups at many colleges.

Another opportunity is becoming involved with organizations such as the GISCorps, which coordinates volunteer projects that benefit underprivileged communities throughout the world. In one 2018 project, volunteers digitally mapped a province in Africa's Democratic Republic of Congo to identify areas with the highest risk for transmission of the poliovirus.

Performing one or more internships is highly recommended for aspiring cartographers. Students usually do internships during

A cartographer collects and analyzes information before creating a map. Mapmaking has grown increasingly sophisticated thanks to interactive and GPS technologies.

the summer months, when school is on break. By interning, they can earn a salary while getting hands-on experience in their chosen field. In a 2016 interview on the Geoawesomeness website, cartographer Mamata Akella talks about falling in love with the field during her first introduction to cartography class. She started spending hours and hours in the lab designing maps and did as many internships as possible in order to learn about mapmaking. "Over the next two years, I made as many maps as I could," says Akella, "and interned at a variety of places who used maps and GIS in different ways."

Skills and Personality

In order to be good at their jobs, cartographers need a wide variety of skills. Critical thinking is essential, as is analytical ability. Cartographers must have a keen eye for detail and a talent for layout and design, as well as be skilled at working with various types of sophisticated software. They must be well organized, able to cope with change, and capable of making good decisions. They also need good interpersonal skills because cartographers frequently consult with others about data and how it is best presented in map form.

On the Job

Employers

Cartographers are employed by a wide variety of industries. BLS reports show that cartographers and photogrammetrists (specialists in making reliable measurements using photographs) together held about 12,600 jobs in 2016. The largest employers were local government agencies, followed by architectural, engineering, and surveying firms. Management, scientific, and technical consulting service firms employ a large number of cartographers, as do state and federal government agencies. According to Purdue University's cartography program website, cartographers who are employed by government agencies work for areas such as highway departments, land management, natural resources planning, and national defense.

Working Conditions

Although cartographers spend much of their time in offices, certain projects require extensive time doing fieldwork to collect data and analyze results. For example, says the BLS, cartographers may travel to the physical locations they are mapping. Doing so can give them a better understanding of the topography of an area, meaning the arrangement of natural and artificial physical features.

Most cartographers work full time and will typically work more than forty hours per week if they are traveling or doing fieldwork. Many who work in this profession say that there is no such thing as a typical day. A cartographer who works for the CIA explains, "Each day is a little different. At any given time, I have eight to ten projects that are at varying stages of development."

Earnings

Cartographers are paid quite well. According to the BLS, as of May 2017 the median annual wage was just under $64,000. That is an average of the lowest-paid 10 percent, who make about $40,300 per year, and the highest-paid 10 percent, who earned more than $100,670.

The federal government paid the highest wages to cartographers as of 2017, with the average annual wage being $89,010. This was followed by management, scientific, and technical consulting services; local government agencies; architectural, engineering, and related services; and state government agencies (in that order).

Opportunities for Advancement

Cartographers who gain work experience, sharpen their technical skills, and earn credibility for being skilled mapmakers may be promoted to higher-level leadership positions. Returning to school to earn a graduate degree will heighten their chances of career advancement.

What Is the Future Outlook for Cartographers?

According to the BLS, cartography and photogrammetry jobs in the United States are expected to grow by 19 percent through 2026, which is among the highest growth rates for all engineering professions. Because cartography is a relatively small field, this 19 percent will result in only about 2,400 new jobs. Still, there are many indications that the future looks bright for aspiring cartographers.

Find Out More

Cartography and Geographic Information Society
PO Box 70006
Albuquerque, NM 87197
website: https://cartogis.org

The Cartography and Geographic Information Society supports research and education to improve the understanding, creation, analysis, and use of maps and geographic information. Its website features archived news releases, information about student scholarships, and a detailed brochure for students titled *Careers in Cartography and GIS*.

GIS Geography

website: https://gisgeography.com

GIS Geography is an information-packed website about geographic information systems and geography, which are topics of great interest to cartographers. The site offers articles about careers in cartography; sections on mapping, satellites, and software; and a search engine that produces numerous articles about cartography.

International Cartographic Association (ICA)

website: https://icaci.org

The ICA seeks to promote the professions of cartography and GIScience (geographic information science) in an international context. Its website features an *eCARTO News* section with archived news articles, a newsletter, abundant information about cartography and its history, cartographic resources, and a maps section with fascinating content.

North American Cartographic Information Society (NACIS)

American Geographical Society Library
2311 E. Hartford Ave.
Milwaukee, WI 53211
website: http://nacis.org

The NACIS is a society of map enthusiasts. Members include specialists from private, academic, and government organizations, as well as other interested individuals. The website features a gallery of maps, information about student map competitions, and a link to the *Cartographic Perspectives* journal.

Biomedical Engineer

What Does a Biomedical Engineer Do?

Biomedical engineers develop solutions to health care problems and needs. By putting to use their knowledge of engineering principles and medical sciences, they design and create a wide variety of instruments and equipment that are used in hospitals, doctors' offices, clinics, and other health care settings. They also develop software designed to run high-tech medical instruments and machines.

Biomedical engineers design and build machines for a wide variety of purposes. X-ray machines, computed tomography scanners, and magnetic resonance imaging machines may be used to diagnose internal abnormalities. Heart-lung machines, also developed by biomedical engineers, oxygenate and pump a patient's blood during open-heart surgery, during which abnormalities can be corrected and diseased valves replaced. Cardiac pacemakers stimulate a dysfunctional heart and restore proper rhythm. Ventilators breathe for patients so that operations can be performed while they are under anesthesia. Biomedical engineers design and build these and other lifesaving machines, train medical personnel in their use, and provide ongoing support and maintenance.

At a Glance

Biomedical Engineer

Minimum Educational Requirements
Bachelor's degree

Personal Qualities
Analytical skills, math proficiency, communication skills, creativity, problem-solving skills

Certification and Licensing
May be required by some employers

Working Conditions
Indoors

Salary Range
About $52,070 to $142,610 per year

Number of Jobs
About 21,300 in 2016

Future Job Outlook
Growth of 7 percent through 2026

Biomedical engineers also design and build machines that can help rehabilitate patients. Amanda Edwards, a biomedical engineer at the University of Virginia, designed an upper-extremity robot. She created the robot to help patients with damage to the cerebellum, which is a part of the brain that coordinates and regulates muscular activity. "When it is damaged, patients exhibit poorly coordinated, oscillatory movements, which is colloquially described as 'moving like they're drunk,'" Edwards explains in a November 2017 interview on the Society of Women Engineers blog. These patients, says Edwards, often have very few treatment options, so she created the robot to help improve their muscular movements.

Along with creating health care machinery, biomedical engineers design and build artificial body parts. They may, for instance, create artificial joints used in knee or hip replacement surgery, or artificial organs such as bladders or heart valves. They also design prosthetic limbs. Susannah Engdahl, a graduate student at the University of Michigan, had a very personal reason for choosing a career in biomedical engineering: She was born without hands and missing most of both feet. The field of biomedical engineering, says Engdahl, was a natural choice for her because it "hit all the checkmarks," meaning health, math, science, and the human body. In an August 2016 University of Michigan news release, Engdahl explains, "Biomedical engineering is a broad field and prosthetics stood out because I already knew how important prosthetics can be in improving quality of life."

Many biomedical engineers work in research and development, conducting research to find solutions to clinical problems. They present their research findings to scientists, clinicians, hospital management, engineers, other colleagues, and the public. They often publish papers that include specific recommendations based on their research findings. Or biomedical engineers may choose to use their knowledge of chemistry and biology to develop new drug therapies, or they may draw on their math and statistics skills to build models that help show how signals are transmitted by the brain or heart.

Biomedical engineers often choose to specialize in a particular area. The specialty of bioinstrumentation, for instance, combines electronics, computer science, and measurement principles to develop instruments used in the diagnosis and treatment of medical problems. One example is sensors used to detect and measure the bodily functions of astronauts in spaceflight, which are then transmitted to researchers on the ground for evaluation. Another biomedical specialty, known as biomaterials, is the study of naturally occurring or laboratory-designed materials that are used in medical devices or as implantation materials. The biomechanics specialty focuses on how the systems and structures of biological organisms—from the tiniest plants to the largest mammals—react to various forces and stimuli.

How Do You Become a Biomedical Engineer?

Education

The Bureau of Labor Statistics (BLS) advises young people who are interested in biomedical engineering to select a high school curriculum that is heavy in science and math. They should take classes in chemistry, physics, and biology, as well as algebra, geometry, trigonometry, and calculus. They will also benefit from taking courses in drafting or mechanical drawing and computer programming.

After high school graduation, aspiring biomedical engineers must attend college and earn a bachelor's degree. To diversify their knowledge, many major in mechanical or electrical engineering and minor in biomedical engineering. Their college curriculum will vary depending on what major they choose but will typically be heavy in mathematics (calculus, statistics, and trigonometry) and sciences (organic chemistry, physics, and molecular biology). Aspiring biochemical engineers may also be advised to take classes in fluid and solid mechanics, computer programming, circuit design, and biomaterials.

Many aspiring biomedical engineers go beyond their bachelor's degree to earn a master's degree or PhD. They can benefit in many ways from higher education, such as being selected for leadership positions with greater responsibilities. Biomedical engineers who hold a master's degree, for instance, might lead a team of researchers, while those who hold a PhD are qualified to teach at a college or university.

Certification

According to the Biomedical Engineering Society, most biomedical engineers are not licensed, although some choose to earn their Professional Engineering (PE) license. Those who do must complete three steps after earning a bachelor's degree from an engineering program accredited by the Accreditation Board for Engineering Technology: pass the Fundamentals of Engineering exam, work for four years under a licensed professional engineer, and earn a passing score on the PE exam. Biomedical engineers who have completed all the necessary qualifications are licensed by the state in which they live.

Volunteer Work and Internships

Aspiring biomedical engineers can find plenty of opportunities for volunteer work, one of which is involvement with clubs and student groups. At Duke University the Biomedical Engineering department offers a seven-week summer program for high school students who are interested in science and engineering. The program was introduced during the summer of 2018. It matched selected students from local public schools with Duke biomedical labs. The students worked on specific projects with mentors and gained insight into what it takes to be an engineer. They learned skills such as using three-dimensional printing and how to develop specialized software.

Career experts and educator advisers stress the importance of internships for aspiring biomedical engineers. These are typically paid positions and often take place during the summer months, when students are on break from school. Closely related to internships are co-op programs, in which students work at a paid job in their chosen field during the school year and earn college credits. Along with gaining valuable work experience, a benefit to both internships and co-op programs is that students have a very good chance of being hired by the companies for whom they have been working.

Skills and Personality

Biomedical engineers need a variety of skills in order to succeed in their careers, with problem-solving skills among the most essential. They must be analytical and able to think creatively, since designing products for health care requires creative problem solving. They need to be mathematically inclined, since in the course of their jobs, biomedical engineers rely on the principles of calculus and other advanced types of math and statistics. They also need self-motivation and good time-management skills.

Personality traits needed by biomedical engineers include patience, a strong work ethic, and good interpersonal skills, including the ability to communicate effectively. These engineers sometimes work with patients and often work on teams, so they must speak well and be good listeners.

On the Job

Employers

According to the BLS, biomedical engineers held 21,300 jobs during 2016. The largest employers that year were medical equipment and supplies manufacturers, who accounted for 22 percent of all biomedical employers. Other top industries that employ biomedical engineers are research and development firms in physical, engineering, and life sciences; navigational, measuring, electromedical, and control instruments manufacturers; state, local, and private colleges, universities, and professional schools; and health care and social assistance groups (in that order).

Working Conditions

Biomedical engineers usually work full time and keep a normal schedule. But, says the BLS, they work additional hours when necessary to meet the needs of patients, managers, colleagues, and clients. One in five biomedical engineers reports working more than forty hours per week.

Where biomedical engineers work depends on what projects they are working on. They may work in an office using a computer to design new instruments or devices. After developing a new medical device, they will likely spend hours in a hospital to monitor the device and ensure that it works as it was designed. Biomedical engineer Sean Pisano is responsible for providing technical expertise on orthopedic medical devices, so he spends a great deal of time in hospital operating rooms. In a 2017 "Biomedical Engineering Success Stories" article on the Ohio State University website, Pisano explains, "Essentially I am making sure the correct products are available and the surgical staff is using them appropriately."

Earnings

Biomedical engineers can earn a very good living. According to the BLS, as of May 2017 these professionals earned an average of $88,040 per year. Wages for the lowest-paid 10 percent were $52,070 per year, and the highest-paid 10 percent earned more than $142,600.

The highest-paying industry for biomedical engineers was research and development in the physical, engineering, and life sciences, which was paying more than $95,000 per year in May 2017. Navigational, measuring, electromedical, and control instruments manufacturers were the second-highest-paying industries, with annual wages of $94,480. Other top-paying employers (in order) include medical equipment and supplies manufacturers; health care and social assistance groups; and colleges, universities, and professional schools, including state, local, and private.

Opportunities for Advancement

Biomedical engineers typically earn greater responsibility as they accumulate experience and pursue higher education. Those who want to lead research teams, for example, typically need a master's degree or higher. Earning a master's degree in business administration may help biomedical engineers move into managerial positions. Another option for those who are interested in research is becoming a medical scientist, a position that requires a PhD in biology or a related life science.

What Is the Future Outlook for Biomedical Engineers?

Employment of biomedical engineers is projected to grow 7 percent through 2026, which is the average for all occupations. This will result in the creation of about fifteen hundred new jobs in the coming years. According to the BLS, biomedical engineers will likely see employment growth because of expanding possibilities from new technologies and their use in creating medical equipment and devices. "Smartphone technology and three-dimensional printing are examples of technology being applied to biomedical advances," says the BLS.

The aging US population is also increasing demand for the work of biomedical engineers. People are living longer and staying more active, and this is likely to increase the demand for biomedical devices and procedures like hip and knee replacements. In the future, says the BLS, biomedical engineers' ability to work in different activities with workers from a variety of fields will enlarge the range of applications for the products and services they design and create.

Find Out More

American Institute for Medical and Biological Engineering (AIMBE)
1400 I St. NW, Suite 235
Washington, DC 20005
website: https://aimbe.org

The AIMBE advocates for the value of medical and biological engineering to society. Its website provides information on public policy, current news, and a special section for students that contains a wealth of information on biomedical engineering, including career advice, education, areas of specialty, and recorded interviews with biomedical engineers.

Biomedical Engineering Society

8201 Corporate Dr., Suite 1125
Landover, MD 20785
website: www.bmes.org

The Biomedical Engineering Society seeks to promote and enhance knowledge and education in biomedical engineering worldwide and its impact on human health and well-being. Publications available on the website include journals, the *Biomedical Engineering News* e-newsletter, and a link to the society's blog.

BME Source

website: www.bmesource.org

This is a shared web portal for anyone involved in (or interested in) the biomedical technology field. Aspiring biomedical engineers can find information about colleges that offer biomedical technology degrees, courses, open positions, and much more.

National Institute of Biomedical Imaging and Bioengineering (NIBIB)

9000 Rockville Pike
Building 31, Room 1C14
Bethesda, MD 20892
website: www.nibib.nih.gov/science-education

An agency of the National Institutes of Health, the NIBIB is dedicated to improving human health by leading the development and application of biomedical technologies. The NIBIB website's search engine produces a wide variety of publications on topics related to biomedical engineering.

Interview with an Environmental Engineer

Lauren Gordon is an environmental engineer with a state government agency in San Luis Obispo, California. She has worked as an environmental engineer for more than seven years. In an interview conducted via e-mail, Gordon provided answers to the author's questions.

Q: Why did you become an environmental engineer?
A: As a child, I lived on a ranch in California with my family. Our drinking water came from a well on our property that would often go dry during the summer time. At a young age, I wanted to learn more about water conservation and how to find more groundwater to be used for drinking water, all over the world. While in college in Montana I studied geological engineering and specialized in hydrogeology (groundwater). One of my professors encouraged me to take a geochemistry class. My college was located in a town that consisted of a very large environmental cleanup site. The town is a large mining town in Montana. I took the geochemistry class and became very interested in environmental cleanup related to mining. The Environmental Protection Agency (EPA) has been working to clean up and rehabilitate that area for over 30 years. I found it to be very interesting and inspiring. So after I graduated from college, I started practicing as an environmental engineer.

Q: Can you describe your typical workday?

A: Currently, I work for a government agency that regulates water quality, including groundwater, surface water, etc. My job is very dynamic and involves participating in discussions relating to regulatory decisions, working with the public, and even conducting some research. I am working on quite a few different projects, which keeps my days different and interesting.

Q: What do you like most about your job?

A: I really enjoy working with such intelligent individuals to make a difference for our environment now and for the future. Generally, I enjoy working with people, and I find the technical aspect of my job to be very interesting as well. In the course of my work, I utilize investigative and problem solving skills, which can be a lot of fun—but it can also be stressful depending on the situation. Environmental engineering has a lot of different aspects. Each industry (agriculture, cleanup, water treatment, mining, petroleum, and regulatory, etc.) has its own challenges and aspects that make it interesting. I like how dynamic this field is, and how as an environmental engineer you have the opportunity to work in many different industries that pose their own problems that need to be solved . . . all in the interest of conserving, rehabilitating or utilizing the environment.

Q: What do you like least about your job?

A: It often takes a long time to see change in the environment even if you are doing a lot of good work. The response of the environment and ecology paired with the slow process of government work can make it very daunting. In the long run, though, you do see positive change and that is very rewarding.

Q: What personal qualities do you find most valuable for this type of work?

A: Enthusiasm, communication, and a willingness to learn. A positive attitude goes a long way in this industry and is important because sometimes the job can be very challenging. Strong communication skills are also important because there can be a lot of moving pieces in your job, working with a variety of people from different industries. It's important to keep an open mind and communicate well.

Q: What is the best way to prepare for this type of job?
A: While in school, try to get as much hands-on experience as possible. Internships, co-ops, and shadowing professionals are all very important activities to take part in. You develop relationships with people in the industry and have exposure to different aspects of the industry that will be very valuable in your career, and especially when you are looking for a job.

Q: What other advice do you have for students who might be interested in becoming an environmental engineer?
A: Environmental engineering is a very broad industry, where you can go many different routes. Do a lot of networking and try out different things before settling on a career path. Fortunately, there are a lot of opportunities out there for environmental engineers, which means there is a lot to explore!

Other Jobs in Engineering

Aerospace engineer
Aerospace engineering and operations technician
Agricultural engineer
Architectural engineer
Automotive engineer
Chemical engineer
Civil engineering technician
Cloud support engineer
Computer hardware engineer
Drafter
Electrical and electronics engineering technician
Electromechanical technician
Engineering support specialist
Entertainment engineer
Environmental engineering technician
Facilities project engineer
Geological engineer
Health and safety engineer
HVAC test technician
Industrial engineering technician
IT technician
Landscape architect
Logistician
Manufacturing technician
Marine engineer/naval architect
Materials engineer
Mechanical engineering technician
Mining engineer
Nuclear engineer
Photogrammetrist
Photonics engineer
Product engineering specialist
Quality engineer
Software engineering support specialist
Surveying and mapping technician
Surveyor
Systems engineering specialist

Editor's Note: The US Department of Labor's Bureau of Labor Statistics provides information about hundreds of occupations. The agency's *Occupational Outlook Handbook* describes what these jobs entail, the work environment, education and skill requirements, pay, future outlook, and more. The *Occupational Outlook Handbook* may be accessed online at www.bls.gov/ooh.

Index